L'ARTISTE

Judy Claxton is a self-taught artist with a passion for rubber stamping, collage and photography. Born in Oklahoma, Judy was first introduced to stamping by a neighbor in American Samoa, where her husband was working. She bought her first heating tool in 1997, starting a love affair with this art form that has lasted to this day.

Many of Judy's unique stamped creations have appeared in *Stampington Inspirations* magazine, for which she works as an "artist on call." When she's not designing in her Redlands, California, studio, she's teaching her techniques at A Little Bizaar, a stamp specialty store in Lake Elsinore, California.

Judy was married to the late David Claxton for 44 years. She has two grown children, four grandchildren and a best friend—her Shih-Tzu dog.

Dedication

I'd like to dedicate this book to the memory of my late husband, David Claxton, who always enthusiastically encouraged and supported my passion for stamping, and who was my biggest fan. And, to my mother, Naomi Cornwell, who also gave me endless encouragement and was thrilled at my every success in art. I love and miss you both.

Acknowledgment

This book came about, in part, due to the support of Laurie Lewis, owner of A Little Bizaar in Lake Elsinore, California. She continually encourages and promotes my work and provides a venue and opportunity for my teaching. I also appreciate my students, who are always a source of joy and inspiration.

Rubber Stamp Gifts. Copyright © 2003 by Judy Claxton. Manufactured in Singapore. All rights reserved. The patterns and drawings in the book are for personal use of the crafter. By permission of the author and publisher, they may be either hand-traced or photocopied to make single copies, but under no circumstances may they be resold or republished. It is permissible for the purchaser to make the projects contained herein and sell them at fairs, bazaars and craft shows. No other part of this book may be reproduced in any form or by any electronic or mechanical means including information storage and retrieval systems without permission in writing from the publisher, except by a reviewer, who may quote a brief passage in review. Published by North Light Books, an imprint of F&W Publications, Inc., 4700 East Galbraith Road, Cincinnati, Ohio 45236. (800) 289-0963. First edition.

07 06 05 04 03 5 4 3 2 1   ISBN 1-58180-466-0

TABLE OF

CONTENTS

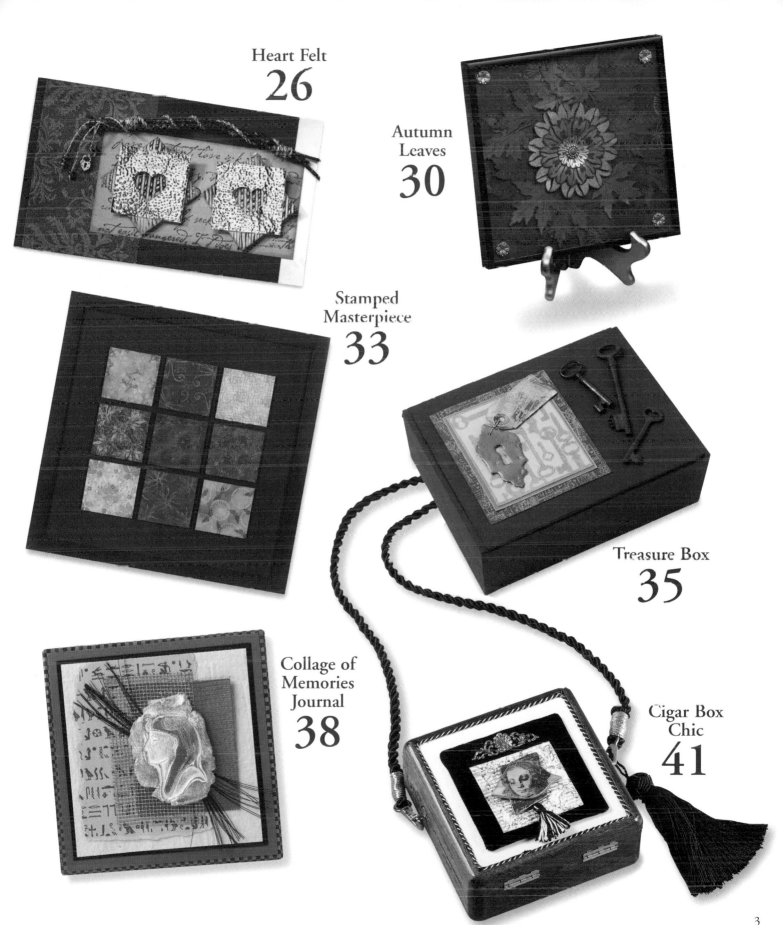

TOOLS AND SUPPLIES

When you go to your local crafts store or a rubber stamping store, you may be overwhelmed and puzzled by the variety of supplies available to stampers. The following is a brief description of some of the supplies and tools that I use. You'll be able to understand their use by reading the descriptions, but the best way to figure out the supplies is to actually use them. There's nothing like experimenting to see how the inks, embossing powders, glazes, and dyes work. I would also encourage you to take classes and to read as many books and magazines on stamping as possible to familiarize yourself with what's available.

Inkpads

Dye inkpads

These are available in pre-inked pads (the traditional stamp pads that you're probably familiar with). They come in a large variety of colors, are water-based and quick drying. These inks are used for stamping on all papers.

Pigment inkpads

These also come in a wide variety of vivid colors. The ink is slow drying so these inks are typically used with embossing powders. The sponges on these pads sit above the base of the container so that they can be used to ink directly to any size stamp (rather than applying the stamp to the pad).

I use small oval stamp pads called Cat's Eyes (from Colorbox) for decorating directly to the paper or directly to a stamp. They're easy to handle, come in lots of colors and are relatively inexpensive.

Inks

Embossing ink

A slow drying, water-based ink used with embossing powders. The ink is applied from a bottle onto a pad, or comes pre-inked on pads. The ink is colorless or slightly tinted.

Re-inkers

Small bottles of dye or embossing inks that can be used to revitalize ink pads. I also use them for watercoloring (just add a little water to the ink) or for painting directly on a stamp and then stamping onto paper. This gives you a loose, arty look.

Permanent ink

This type of ink is for nonporous surfaces such as glass or wood. You can either use permanent ink stamp pads or make your own by cutting a small piece of felt and placing it on a disposable plastic plate that can be thrown away when you're finished stamping.

Embossing powders

Embossing powders give dimension to your work. The powder blends with the ink and adheres to the stamped surface when heated with a heat gun. Embossing powders are available in a myriad of colors including metallic and clear varieties.

Heat gun

You'll want to invest in a really good heat gun. This is used for all of your embossing, so you'll be using it quite a bit. The heat gun is hand-held, and heat is applied directly to the stamped surface. A gun holder is also a handy thing to have on hand.

Note: A hair dryer does not get hot enough to melt embossing powder.

Decorating chalks

I use decorating chalks by Craf'T Products to shade and blend colors for a soft pastel finish. Applied with their sponge applicators, the chalks can be layered or worked together to achieve a third color. They're acid free and non toxic.

Dry brush markers

Markers can be used to color your stamped project on paper or you can color your rubber stamp directly with the marker (rather than using a stamp pad). Markers are especially useful when you want a multicolored look. You can use several different colors to paint directly on your stamp and then stamp to paper.

Metallic markers

I use metallic markers that are available in gold, silver, bronze, etc.

I especially like a gold leafing pen for adding borders to cards, writing a personal message, or for decorating a stamped polymer or air-dry clay image.

Adhesives

Glue sticks

As you will see in the following projects, I use a glue stick for almost all my layering of paper.

Craft glues

I use either Yes brand or the The Ultimate Glue for adding embellishments such as charms, polymer clay pieces, beads, etc. They dry clear and are easy to clean up.

Double-sided tape

This tape is used for layering paper and adding bits and scraps of paper to a project. It's not as permanent as glue and it tends to melt when heated.

Dimensional glue

Diamond Glaze is a water-based dimensional adhesive that I use in my work. It can be used directly over artwork for a raised, glass-like finish, or when thinned with water, a lacquer-like finish. Dye ink can be added to it to achieve custom colors. It's also used for gluing glitter, beads, glass, plastic and vellum to paper.

Additional supplies:

Hole punch
Decorative punches
Craft knife
Instant coffee
Glitter glue
Metal ruler
Scissors
Scotch tape
Tweezers
Large drinking glass or PVC pipe
   for rolling out clays

INTRODUCTION

Speaking as one who has always been very art oriented, I think of rubber stamping as a unique art form rather than a craft. Stamps give you the opportunity to create fine art, even if you're not proficient at drawing or painting. You can use rubber stamps and pigments to create beautiful framed artwork, greeting cards and gifts beyond compare. There is just no limit to what you can do with stamps—embellish boxes, decorate candles, even make a purse from a cigar box.

This how-to book is geared toward the beginning stamper who wants to move a bit beyond the basics. I'll show you how to create amazing wall and table art and, of course, make some gorgeous cards. As an experienced stamp artist, I still love to make cards, but mine have

evolved into dramatic art miniatures that can be framed or used to decorate other objects. I also enjoy making art books, which can be displayed on a coffee table or presented in place of a greeting card.

You'll find that some projects in this book look somewhat complicated, but rest assured, they're simple to create. My students are often astonished at how easy it is to put together a project they were sure was difficult. If you can follow a good recipe, you can follow my step-by-step instructions and achieve wonderful results.

Stamping changed my world, and I love it from the bottom of my heart. I hope you will too!

GENERAL INSTRUCTIONS

Inking a stamp

Apply the stamp on the dye-based pad. Then stamp it on a test piece of paper. Check to see that it stamped completely and that you didn't get any edges from the untrimmed part of the stamp. Keep trying until you get a nice clean image. Re-ink your stamp again and stamp on your project.

Another way to ink your stamp is with a colored marker. Color the complete image area or only part of the image.

Or use different colored markers on the stamp for a multi-colored look.

When using the extra large stamps (such as a texture stamp or script stamp) on a small project, you can ink your stamp and place your project directly onto the stamp to ink it.

Direct to paper inking technique

Use your stamp pad to decorate the paper. It must be a raised pad (such as Cat's Eyes from Colorbox). Gently rub the pad onto the paper or use a sponge. You can use more than one color to create different looks.

Embossing

To achieve a dimensional look to your project, first apply embossing ink to your stamp. Embossing ink is usually clear or slightly tinted. The embossing ink can either be on a pad or in a roller tube that you just roll onto your stamp. Then impress the image onto the surface.

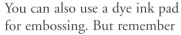

Pour or shake embossing powder over the ink. Shake off the excess into a plastic bag or jar.

Heat the surface using your heat gun until the powder melts and becomes raised.

You can also use a dye ink pad for embossing. But remember that this ink dries a lot faster, so you have to work a little more quickly.

I really encourage you to experiment with embossing. You can use different colors of powders, metallics, even psychedelic glittering powders. You can mix colors of powders together to achieve different effects. Embossing powders are available in different grades from detail, fine to double thick.

GENERAL INSTRUCTIONS

Staining and aging

There are several ways to achieve an aged look to your paper such as:

Direct to paper: Rub on dye ink with the pad or your finger (golds and browns work well).

Coffee: Brush on coffee using a paintbrush. Either brush it all over the paper or brush it in streaks. The same look can be achieved using Walnut Ink Crystals by PostModern Designs.

Torn edges: A nice aged look is achieved when paper is torn around the edges. The torn edges can be left alone or colored with a pen or ink pad.

Polymer clay

Polymer clays come in a variety of colors. The clay can be rolled flat and impressed with stamp images, then baked in an oven. There are molds available to make various shapes.

After baking the clay, it can be painted, glazed or embossed. Then the shape can be glued to cards, journals, albums, or boxes. Polymer clay can also be made into beads.

Air-dry clay

This clay can be decorated the same as poly clays, except it is air dried. It's lighter weight so is useful for decorating cards. The clay can be decorated with markers or colored pencils, as well as with paints.

Using acetate

Decorating cards or journals with stamped acetate is a special technique (see page 14 for example). Stamp your image directly on the acetate. To enhance the stamping, you may wish to add paint. Drip or pour small amounts of paint on the back of the stamped piece of acetate. Marbleize the paint by swirling through it with a chop stick or craft stick. Then apply tissue paper over the top of the paint. Trim tissue to the size of the acetate. Glue the tissue side to your project. Experiment with different colors and types of paint.

Keeping your stamps clean

There are several stamp cleaning solutions available. They remove ink without harming the surface of the stamp. A soft bristle brush can be used to remove dried ink on the stamp.

Tips on using this book

I have given the measurements for all the cardstock or paper that will be used in each project in the materials list. This will make it easier for you to cut all of your paper first before starting your project. You don't have to make your projects exactly the same as mine. You may revise any of the projects as you wish. The step-by-step instructions will lead you through each project.

In the index, we have pictured every stamp that was used in the book along with the manufacturer, which should make it easy for you to locate the stamps used in the various projects.

Your local craft and rubber stamp stores carry complete lines of stamps and supplies, and you may find the stamps you're looking for there. If not, consult the manufacturer, and they will be able to direct you to the store in your area where their stamps are sold.

FALLING LEAVES

I love the delicate beauty of a skeleton leaf, whether naturally green or colored in a different, surprising shade. Purple is my favorite hue, but any color serves to transform this type of leaf into an arty centerpiece.

The stamped, embossed border of this greeting card combines purple and green ink for a leafy cascade, and coordinating cardstock colors tie the look together.

This is a very simple project, but the card is stunning, with an air of sophisticated understatement. You could use this design for a gift set of note cards, or just make an exquisite, special-occasion greeting card for a "VIP" in your life. Both male and female can appreciate this classic design.

Materials:

Ivory cardstock, 5" x 7¹/₂" (12cm x 19cm), 4¹/₄" x 7" (11cm x 18cm), 2¹/₂" x 5¹/₂" (6.5cm x 14cm)

Green cardstock, 4¹/₂" x 7¹/₄" (11cm x 18cm), 3" x 6" (7.5cm x 15cm)

Purple cardstock, 2³/₄" x 5³/₄" (7cm x 14.5cm)

Leaf rubber stamp

Purple and Honeydew metallic ink (Encore stamp pads by Tsukineko)

Clear embossing powder

Skeleton leaf

Small sponge

Glue stick

1. Color the skeleton leaf by applying purple metallic ink with a small sponge. (Note: Skeleton leaves can also be found already dyed.)

2. Stamp leaf image around the edge of the medium ivory piece of cardstock using the Honeydew ink.

3. Emboss with clear embossing powder. (See embossing instructions page 3.) Shake off excess powder into the container to save for future use.

4. Stamp the leaf image using the purple ink in between and overlapping some of the green leaf images. Emboss these images using the clear embossing powder and heat with heat gun.

5. Layer the card according to the diagram below using a glue stick.

6. To finish, glue the leaf to the center of the card using the glue stick.

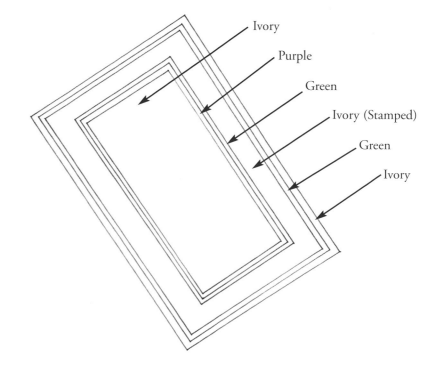

Ivory

Purple

Green

Ivory (Stamped)

Green

Ivory

CANDLE NECKLACE

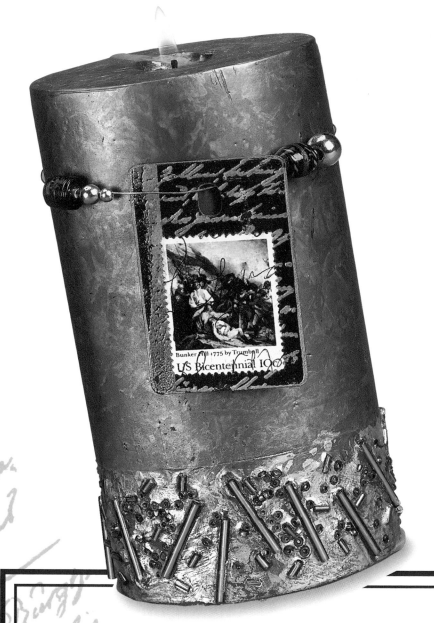

Home improvement stores offer free sample chips of countertop material. These small, durable tags can be put to good use by a creative stamp artist. These terrific mini-canvases feature a hole near the top, allowing you to hang your potential masterpiece on a decorative candle or other object. You can even wear the finished product as a pendant on a cord or chain around your neck.

I decorated this sample with a beautiful script image. An artistic postage stamp adds a colorful accent and this simple project is complete! Hung on a strand of bead-embellished wire, the piece adds interest to a decorative pillar candle, which finds new status as an object d'art.

This is a great gift idea for a friend. Make several—the possibilities are endless!

Materials:

Countertop sample chip
Script rubber stamp
Gold pigment ink (Color Box)
Gold embossing powder
Heat gun
Postage stamp
Glue stick

Craft glue
6 to 8 assorted beads
Gold bugle and seed beads
24-gauge gold wire
Bronze pillar candle
Silver acrylic paint

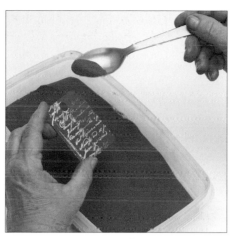

1. Apply the gold pigment ink directly to the stamp. Press the sample chip onto the inked part of the stamp.

2. While the ink is still wet, sprinkle gold embossing powder over the image. With a heat gun, emboss the image (see page 3 for embossing instructions).

3. Attach the postage stamp to the chip using a glue stick. See photo for placement.

4. Thread various coordinating beads onto the gold wire along with the decorated chip.

5. Wrap the wire around the candle and twist in back to secure. Trim excess wire.

If desired, decorate the candle further by applying a band of silver acrylic paint around the bottom portion. When the paint is dry, add gold bugle and seed beads using craft glue.

LEONARDO'S MUSE

Combining unique images, colored papers and several interesting decorative techniques, this is definitely not your basic greeting card. The piece is very aesthetic, with an aura of mystery, almost like a puzzle.

The intriguing Leonardo De Vinci portrait stamp is reproduced on acetate, the back glazed and painted in three colors. The scene also includes a surprising element—a butterfly stamped onto a watch face. To achieve the faux paste-paper look, the paper is hand-painted and combed, then gold glitter is added for an ethereal glow.

This makes a stunning gift card and is definitely suitable for framing. The meaning? It's in the eye of the beholder!

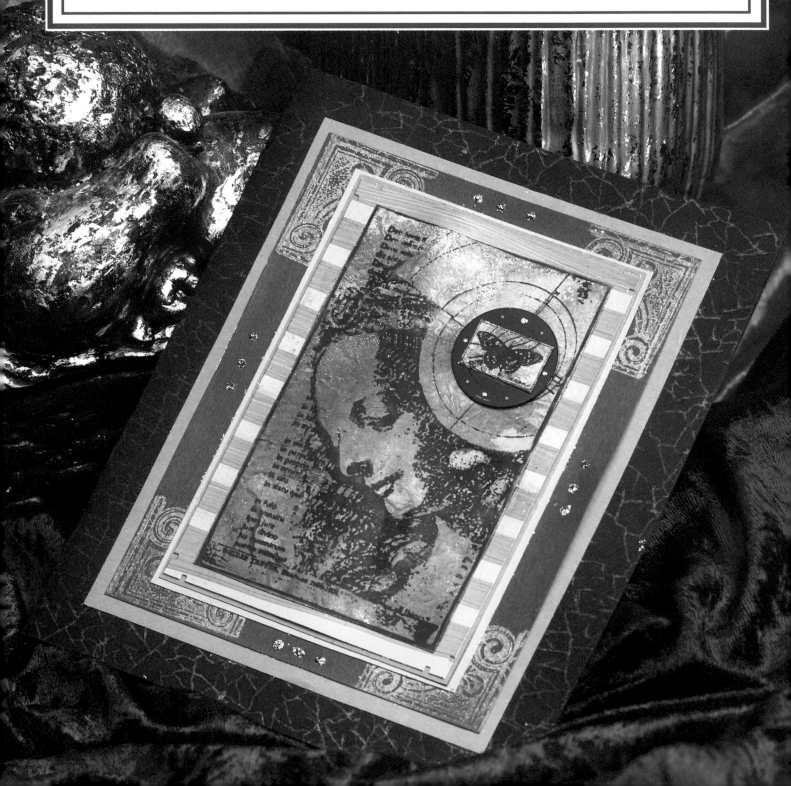

Materials:

Black cardstock,
6¼" x 10½" (16cm x 27cm)
Light purple cardstock,
4¼" x 5½" (11cm x 14cm),
3⅛" x 4⅝" (8cm x 11.5cm)
Gold cardstock,
3¼" x 4¾" (8.3cm x 12cm),
3" x 4½" (7.5cm x 11cm)
Dark purple cardstock,
4" x 5¼" (10cm x 13cm),
2½" x 4" (6cm x 10cm)
Acetate, 2¼" x 4" (6.5cm x 10cm)

Crackle, corner image, woman,
  butterfly rubber stamps
Gold pigment ink (Colorbox)
Permanent black ink stamp pad
Gold glitter glue
Purple, Gold, Green paint (Lumiere)
Combing tool
Heat gun
Dimensional glue (Diamond Glaze)
Small craft stick
Tissue paper
Black watch face
Craft glue

1. Fold black cardstock in half. Stamp the crackle image to the black card using the gold pigment ink.

2. Stamp each corner of the larger piece of dark purple cardstock with the corner stamp and gold pigment ink. Apply three small dots to the four sides of the card using gold glitter glue (see photo for placement).

3. Apply Green paint to the small piece of gold cardstock on one end and comb through to the other side to create stripes. Set aside to dry.

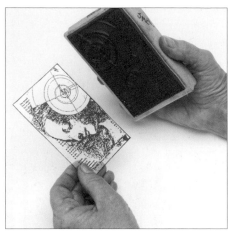

4. Stamp the image of the woman on the acetate using a black ink stamp pad. Heat set using a heat gun so that the ink will dry quickly.

5. Apply a small amount of dimensional glue on the reverse side of the acetate and spread it over the entire surface. (Tip: Use an old credit card to spread the glaze evenly.) Pour small amounts of Purple, Green and Gold paint over the glue.

6. Run a small craft stick or a chop stick through the paint to marbleize it. Don't mix the colors too much or they will become muddy.

Using a glue stick or double-sided tape, layer the card according to the diagram below.

7. Apply a piece of crumpled tissue paper over the top of the paint. Allow to dry. Trim the tissue to the size of the acetate.

8. Stamp the butterfly image to a small piece of acetate using black ink. Heat set and let dry. Paint Gold on the acetate, cut out, then glue to the watch face. Glue the watch face to the card as pictured.

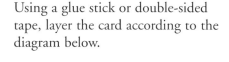

Acetate

Gold

Lt. Purple

Gold

Dk. Purple

Lt. Purple

Black

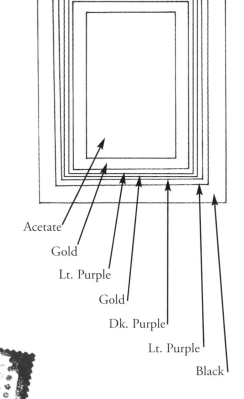

POCKETFUL OF MEMORIES

Some people capture memories and feelings through words, but if you're like me, you prefer more visual forms of self expression. This exquisite little booklet is my sonnet, created as a tribute to my favorite city, Paris.

I included a few charms, faux gold leafing and other surprises and also created a matching envelope purse to hold the book.

I love the look of the stained paper on both pieces   it adds another dimension and rich, rustic color.

This creative set offers an artistic tour of Paris, and a wonderful conversation piece. Create your own little travel souvenir, or send a friend off with a commemorative bon voyage gift.

POCKETFUL OF
MEMORIES

Materials:

Ivory paper,
   8¹/₂" x 14" (22cm x 36cm),
   8¹/₂" x 11" (22cm x 28cm)
Various travel rubber stamps
Brown, red and gold ink stamp pads
Clear embossing ink stamp pad
Clear embossing powder
Paintbrush
Coffee or walnut stain
Ruler and pencil
Craft knife

Sewing machine and thread
Hole punch
1 yd. (91cm) gold metallic cord
12" (30cm) gold metallic thread
Various gold charms
Postage stamps
Sealing wax and seal
2 round amber transparent beads
Heat gun
Craft glue

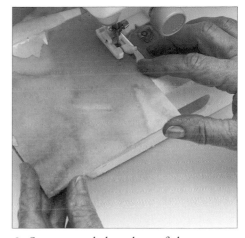

1. Stain both pieces of ivory paper (for the purse and the booklet) using a paintbrush and stain (either coffee or walnut stain). See page 3 for staining. Allow to dry.

2. Cut the large piece following the pattern on page 44 using a straight-edge and craft knife. Fold this piece according to dotted lines on pattern.

3. Sew around the edges of the purse using a sewing machine. You may wish to hand stitch the edges.

Stamp your chosen images on the purse using the brown ink.

(Note: Stamping of images can either be done before or after sewing the purse.)

For a glossy finish, wipe a clear embossing pad on the surface, sprinkle with clear embossing powder and heat with a heat gun.

4. Punch holes (where indicated on pattern) and thread the gold cord through each side of the purse. Knot and trim ends of cord.

19

  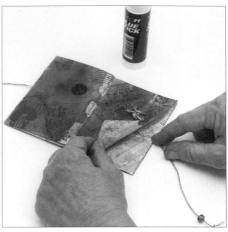

4. For the booklet, fold the smaller stained paper in half lengthwise. Then fold into fourths so that it measures 2³/₄" x 4¹/₄" (7cm x 11cm). Unfold and cut a slit where indicated (see diagram below) using a craft knife.

After cutting the slit in paper, refold it in half. Hold each end of the paper and push the ends together as shown above.

5. Keep pushing the paper until it forms the pages for your book. Stamp desired images to the pages of the book in an artistic and interesting manner. Use a variety of colored inks such as browns, golds and reds. Emboss the front and back covers as in step 3 (page 19) for a glossy finish.

Use craft glue to add small charms, postage stamps and sealing wax stamps to the front of the booklet and on the pages.

6. Cut the gold thread into two 6" (15cm) pieces. Thread a bead onto each piece of thread and tie one end of each piece in a knot. Tape the unknotted end of the thread to the inside center edge of the front cover. Cut a small slit in the folded edge of the back cover, insert the thread and tape on the inside. Tie the thread to close the booklet. Place the booklet inside the purse.

cut

WEDDING ALBUM

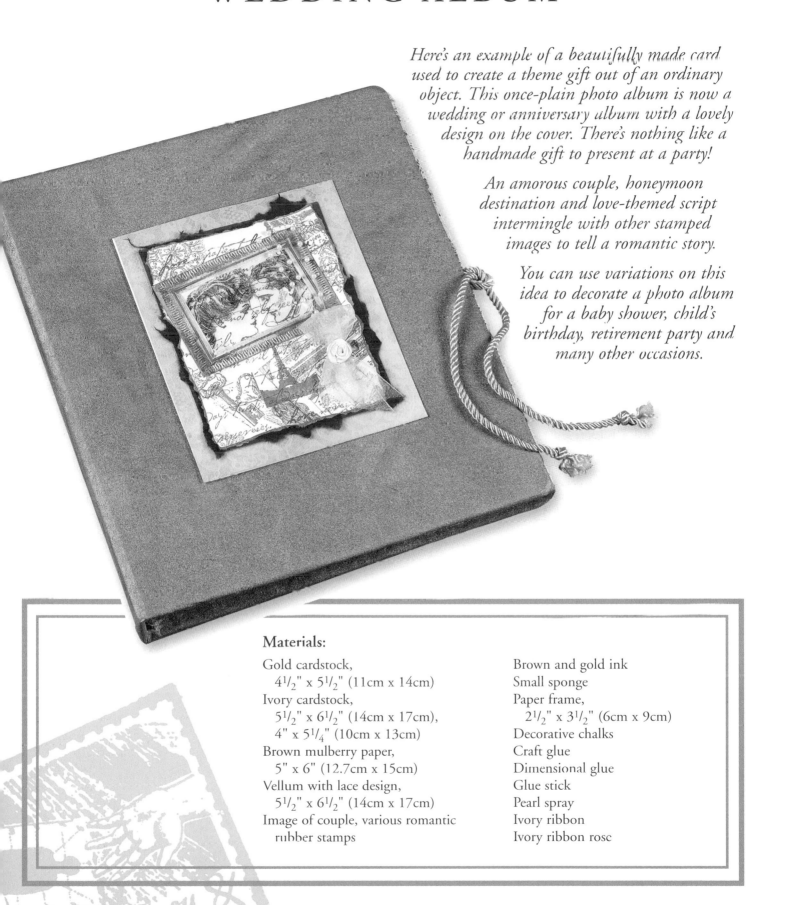

Here's an example of a beautifully made card used to create a theme gift out of an ordinary object. This once-plain photo album is now a wedding or anniversary album with a lovely design on the cover. There's nothing like a handmade gift to present at a party!

An amorous couple, honeymoon destination and love-themed script intermingle with other stamped images to tell a romantic story.

You can use variations on this idea to decorate a photo album for a baby shower, child's birthday, retirement party and many other occasions.

Materials:

Gold cardstock,
    $4^1/_2$" x $5^1/_2$" (11cm x 14cm)
Ivory cardstock,
    $5^1/_2$" x $6^1/_2$" (14cm x 17cm),
    4" x $5^1/_4$" (10cm x 13cm)
Brown mulberry paper,
    5" x 6" (12.7cm x 15cm)
Vellum with lace design,
    $5^1/_2$" x $6^1/_2$" (14cm x 17cm)
Image of couple, various romantic
    rubber stamps

Brown and gold ink
Small sponge
Paper frame,
    $2^1/_2$" x $3^1/_2$" (6cm x 9cm)
Decorative chalks
Craft glue
Dimensional glue
Glue stick
Pearl spray
Ivory ribbon
Ivory ribbon rose

1. Using a small sponge, rub brown ink on the back of the vellum to give it an antiqued look.

2. Tear around the edges of the brown mulberry paper.

3. Stamp the image of the couple toward the top of the smaller piece of ivory cardstock using the brown ink. Stamp the various romantic images around the couple. Using the chalks, color the couple image only.

4. Glue the gold frame over the couple using a glue stick.

5. Apply dimensional glue over the couple within the borders of the frame. If desired, tear around the edges of this piece.

6. Layer and glue all pieces according to the photo above.

7. Glue on the various embellishments including the pearl spray and ribbon, with the ribbon rose over the top. Glue the completed piece to the top of the album.

Note:

If you prefer to to make this into a wedding or anniversary card instead of a decoration for an album, follow the same instructions as above, but cut the larger ivory cardstock to 9" x 5 1/2" (23cm x 14cm) and fold in half.

GOIN' WEST

Whether for a genuine cowboy or the urban variety, this western-themed gift is one answer to the question, "What can I make for the man in my life?"

This decorative tin is just the right size for the booklet tucked inside, and can also hold coins, business cards or cufflinks. Originally a mint tin, its new, leather-like texture is created with clay and then hand rubbed to a gleaming gold.

The booklet is stamped in natural hues decorating the front and back cover. Inside is a collage of images depicting the romantic Old West. A hand-written message or poem can be added, if desired, or simply let the artwork speak for itself!

GOIN' WEST

Materials:

Book board, 2 pieces
  2" x 3" (5cm x 7.5cm)
Kraft paper,
  $2^3/_4$" x 11" (7cm x 28cm),
  2 pieces cut to 3" x 4"
  (8cm x 10cm)

Diamond pattern, various
  western rubber stamps
Black polymer clay
  (Sculpey III)
Gold Mini Metallic Rub Ons
Brown, black and russet
  dye-based ink pads
Mints tin

PVC pipe cut to 6" (15cm)
  or a small rolling pin
Craft knife
Sponge
Craft glue
24" (61cm) twine
Cowboy boot, stars,
  bucking bronco charms

1. To cover the tin, condition clay according to manufacturer's instructions. Roll out the clay using the PVC pipe or a rolling pin to a size slightly larger than the tin.

2. When the clay is approximately $^1/_8$" (0.32cm) thick, stamp it using the diamond design stamp for texture.

3. Wrap the stamped piece of clay on the top and bottom portion of the tin. Press the clay in place and trim where necessary using a craft knife.

4. With a piece of the leftover clay, form four small oval shapes for the feet of the tin. Press the oval "feet" to each corner of the bottom of the tin. Bake the tin in the oven (following manufacturer's instructions).

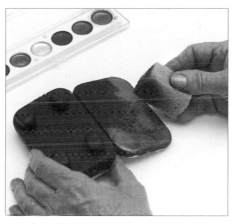

5. After the tin is cool, use the gold Mini Metallic Rub Ons and a sponge to cover the top and bottom of the tin for an aged look.

6. Wrap the twine into a rope shape and wrap another small piece around the top of rolled rope and glue to secure. Glue the rope to the tin. Glue the cowboy boot over the top of the rope. Glue the stars as pictured.

7. Booklet: Scrunch up the two small pieces of kraft paper, then flatten them. Sponge brown and russet ink on the paper. Stamp the images using black ink.

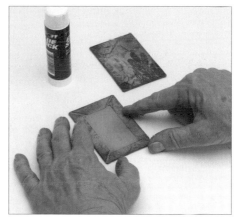

8. Cover the two bookboard pieces with the decorated pieces of paper.

9. Color the pages of the long piece of kraft paper as in step 7. Stamp the various western images in black. Fold the kraft paper like an accordion.

10. Glue the pages to each covered book board piece to form the booklet.

HEART FELT

Whoever receives this gleaming ode to enduring love will never doubt the depth of your feelings!

I don't make many Valentine or romantic cards, but this one is very special—an artistic expression of heartfelt love. It's different, with masculine appeal rather than a cute or frilly feel.

I created this card with my late husband in mind, the true love of my life. The two metal hearts are entwined, or "branched" together, by the twigs above, which are bound with a winding gold cord. The stamped script is from 1 Corinthians:13, the "love chapter" of the Bible, which speaks to ultimate love.

This card is not difficult to create, and it's a keepsake he'll always treasure.

HEART FELT

Materials:

Ivory cardstock,
   $4^1/_2$" x $7^1/_2$" (11cm x 19cm)
Red cardstock, $4^1/_2$" x 7" (11cm x 18cm)
Beige cardstock,
   $2^3/_4$" x $5^1/_2$" (7cm x 13.5cm)
Red small patterned paper, 2 pieces
   $1^3/_4$" (4.5cm) square
Red larger patterned cardstock,
   $4^1/_2$" x 3" (11cm x 7.5cm)
Gold foil, 2 pieces $1^3/_4$" (4.5cm)
 square
Text design rubber stamp

Red dye-based ink
Gold pigment ink
Thin twigs, approximately
   6" (15cm) long
Gold glitter glue
18" (46cm) gold cord
12" (30cm) gold thread
Assorted charms and beads
Heart paper punch
Stylus
Glue stick
Craft glue

1. Apply the gold glitter glue to each twig until they have a shimmering appearance. Allow to dry.

2. Punch up small twigs and wrap them together using the gold cord. Tie and knot the cord on one end and then wrap it around the length of the twigs. Tie and knot on the other end.

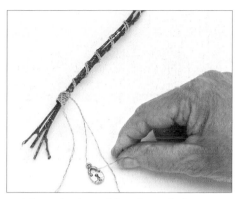

3. Thread selected beads and charms onto three or four strands of thin gold thread. Tie the strands to one end of the twig, knot and trim. Set aside.

4. Punch each square of gold foil in the center using the heart punch.

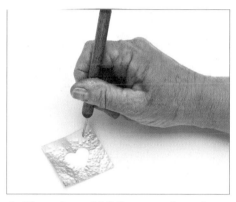

5. Place the gold foil on a soft surface (an opened up phone book works great). Stipple each square by using the small end of a stylus, making pouncing indentations over the foil.

6. Stamp the text image on the beige paper using the red pigment ink stamp pad. Rub the edges of the paper and the small red squares with the gold pigment ink pad for an aged look.

7. Using a glue stick, glue the large patterned red paper to the left edge of the red solid paper. Then glue the text-stamped paper over the red paper. Glue the two red squares diagonally on top of the stamped paper.

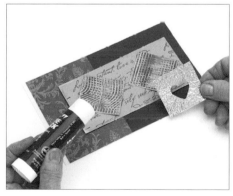

8. Glue the gold foil squares over the top of the red squares (as pictured).

9. Affix the twig arrangement to the top section of the card using craft glue. Then glue this arrangement to the ivory cardstock (the base of the card) using a glue stick.

AUTUMN LEAVES

This is one of those stamp art projects that can leave the average person perplexed, even dumbfounded. "I can't believe you did that with rubber stamps," is a frequent refrain, and I certainly can't blame the skeptics. This framed leaf collage really doesn't look like it was done with stamps, but, indeed, it was.

Sharp scissors play a prominent role here, because each of the stamped leaves and center medallion "petals" have been carefully cut out of cardstock. My special cutting technique contributes to the realistic effect of the paper curling and laying just so.

Displayed on a gold easel, this framed ode to autumn colors is a beautiful piece of table art, as well as a fun conversation piece.

AUTUMN LEAVES

Materials

Black cardstock,
   8" x 8" (20cm x 20cm),
   2 pieces 8$\frac{1}{2}$" x 11" (22cm x 28cm)
Medallion, tree and leaf rubber stamps
Platinum, Verdigris, Quick Silver,
   Gold Rush, Burnt Copper pigment
   inks (Colorbox Metalextra)
Embossing powder (JudiKins
   Psychedelic)

Heat gun
Small, sharp scissors
Double-sided foam tape
Craft glue
Glue stick
5 gold buttons
8" x 8" (20cm x 20cm) frame

1. For the background, stamp the tree and the leaf images randomly over the smaller piece of black cardstock. Use a combination of the metallic colors as desired. Set aside.

2. On the large piece of black cardstock, stamp small medallion with Platinum, the medium with Goldrush and the large with Verdigris. While wet, sprinkle the large medallion with Psychedelic embossing powder and heat with the heat gun. When dry, cut out the medallions, then cut along the lines between each petal.

3. Layer the medallions, small to large, on the center of the background piece. Use glue in the middle of each piece only. With a tweezers apply the double-sided foam tape under the petals to add dimension.

4. Stamp leaf images on the larger piece of black cardstock and color them with Verdigris and Burnt Copper. Cut out each leaf.

5. Arrange the cut out leaves around the medallions alternating the colors as desired. Loosely glue each leaf to the background.

6. Glue one button in the middle of the medallion and one in each corner using craft glue. (If your buttons have shanks on them, cut them off.) Place the completed piece in the frame.

This project was originally taught by Sandi Obertin of Rubber Nature Art Stamps. Shown here with permission.

STAMPED MASTERPIECE

This piece hangs in my home, and frequently inspires a dilemma. Do I keep quiet at exclamations over hours of labor spent, or admit the truth? What looks like an intricate example of abstract art is really very simple— a technique I sometimes even refer to as "mindless stamping."

It isn't really mindless, but it is an exercise in free-play. After choosing your pigment ink palette, you simply lose yourself in a process of

sponge painting and pattern combining using myriad tiny stamps.

Nine foam squares are covered with different pieces of decorated cardstock and arranged together on a black background. It's a great creative outlet, and you end up with a striking abstract for the wall.

If you'd like to make a series of gifts for friends, similar yet unique, this piece may be just what you're looking for.

Materials:

Black foam core, 9 pieces
   3" x 3" (7.5cm x 7.5cm),
   1 piece 12" x 12"
   (30cm x 30cm)
Wine cardstock, 5 pieces
   3" x 3" (7.5cm x 7.5cm)
Parchment cardstock, 4 pieces
   3" x 3" (7.5cm x 7.5cm)
Various pigment inks,
   Colorbox Cat Eyes
Various rubber stamps
Glue stick
Frame, 15" x 15"

1. With pigment ink, use the direct to paper technique (see page 3) to color the squares of cardstock as desired.

2. Rub on a second color. Continue coloring all of the squares using the colors of your choice.

3. Decorate the squares using various images and colors of your choice. Patterned and abstract images work best for this project.

4. Glue the stamped squares to the foam core squares using a glue stick.

5. Position and attach the 9 squares on the large foam core piece (refer to the photograph for placement). Place the finished piece in the frame.

Note:

Kits of this project are available from Magenta. The kit includes precut cardboard (eliminating the cutting steps) with enough supplies for two complete framable artworks. Use your own stamps to create one-of-a-kind masterpieces. See source list, page 47 for information. The project is shown here with permission.

TREASURE BOX

I love the bold colors in this project and the idea of a treasure box decorated with a lock-and-key theme. Antique keys have such a pleasing, elegant shape. I had great fun here indulging a whim to go key crazy!

It's easy to be fooled by the "lock" on the card, but it's made of cardstock, not brass. The stamped cut-out is painted with gold pigment ink and gold embossed. More touches of metallic gold give this a gleaming quality.

This is another example of a stamped card lending beauty and personality to an object, in this case a painted cigar box. A few added embellishments in the form of antique keys and this treasure box is completely, irresistibly unique.

TREASURE BOX

Materials

Red cardstock, 2 pieces
 $4^3/_4$" x $5^1/_4$" (12cm x 13cm)
Orange cardstock, 4" x $4^1/_2$"
 (10cm x 11.5cm)
Gold cardstock, $3^3/_4$" x $4^1/_4$"
 (9.5cm x 10.8cm)
Lock and keys rubber stamps
Red, orange and yellow
 dye-based inks
Gold pigment ink pad

Gold embossing powder
Gold ultra thick embossing powder
Gold leafing pen
Shipping tag and gold thread
Small hole punch
Small sponge
Cigar box
Antique keys
Glue stick
Glue gun and glue sticks

1. Apply red, orange and yellow inks to the shipping tag using a small sponge. Stamp various key images to the tag and emboss with gold embossing powder. (See embossing instructions, page 3.)

2. Stamp the lock image to one piece of red cardstock using a gold pigment ink pad. Set aside.

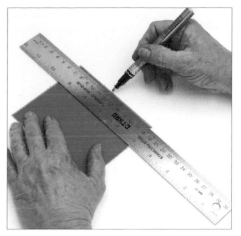

3. Stamp the other red piece with key images and gold pigment ink pad and emboss. Use the gold leafing pen to draw a thin line around the edge of the orange piece and the gold piece. Stamp the gold piece with the key images and emboss.

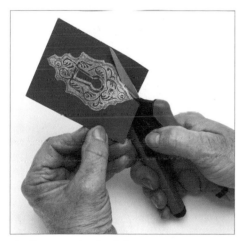

4. Cut out the lock image.

5. Rub on clear embossing ink and emboss using the ultra thick gold embossing powder. Punch a hole near the top of the lock and attach the shipping tag using gold thread.

6. Layer all the elements as pictured above. Glue the finished piece to a painted cigar box and add antique keys using a glue gun to embellish.

Note:

If you'd like to make this into a greeting card (a house-warming card, for instance), follow the same instructions as above, but cut the red cardstock to 9 $\frac{1}{2}$" x 5 $\frac{1}{4}$" (24cm x 13cm) and fold in half.

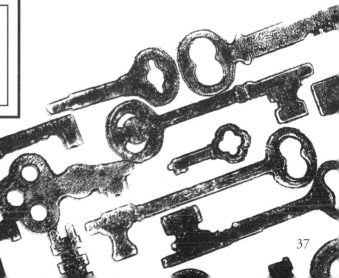

COLLAGE OF MEMORIES JOURNAL

Many people put together a photo album or travel diary after they've toured an exotic locale. As an artist, I tend to think differently about creating a book to commemorate a wonderful trip.

This journal combines stamped patterns and images with several other unique elements to tell the story of a journey to Egypt. It includes faux snakeskin, peacock feathers, clay and sequins—it's great fun selecting just the right creative accessory for the mood you want to achieve. One page features golden door handles made of painted, cut-up chopsticks and metal washers.

You could make a similar journal for Africa, China, Ireland—any country that has inspired you! This makes a wonderful gift for a fellow traveler and a striking coffee-table art book.

Materials

Book board, 2 pieces 6^1/$_2$" x 6^1/$_2$"
(17cm x 17cm)

Wrapping paper, 4 pieces 7" x 7"
(18cm x 18cm)

Brown cardstock, 6" x 6"
(15cm x 15cm)

Black cardstock, 5^1/$_2$" x 5^1/$_2$"
(14cm x 14 cm)

Beige cardstock, 5^1/$_4$" x 5^1/$_4$"
(13cm x 13cm)

Tan cardstock, 4" x 5"
(10cm x 12.7cm)

Purple metallic paper, 2^3/$_4$" x 3^3/$_4$"
(7cm x 9cm)

Mesh, 2^1/$_2$" x 4^1/$_4$" (6cm x 11cm)

Ivory paper, 6" x 24" (15cm x 61cm)

Hieroglyphic, Egyptian queen rubber
stamps

Clear embossing ink

Black ink stamp pad

Air-dry clay

Halo Violet Gold, Pearl Violet metallic
acrylics (Lumiere)

Paintbrush

Animal whiskers (from craft stores)

Heat gun

Craft glue

Elastic cord

1. Roll out a small piece of air-dry clay. Stamp the Egyptian face image onto the clay. Allow to dry. (Tip: Place it on a rack for quick and even drying.)

2. Paint the image using the metallic acrylic paints as desired.

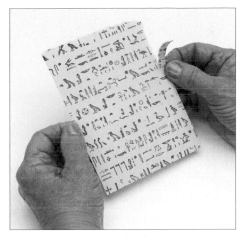

3. Stamp the hieroglyphic image to the beige cardstock using black ink. Tear around the edges of the stamped paper.

4. Apply clear embossing ink over the piece of mesh. Sprinkle with gold embossing powder and heat.

5. Cover both sides of each piece of book board with the metallic checkered wrapping paper.

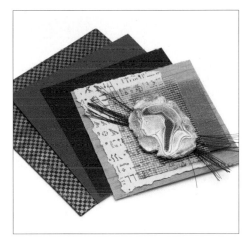

6. Layer all the pieces for the cover of the journal as pictured above.

7. To make the pages for the journal, accordion fold the ivory paper into four 6" (15cm) pages.

8. Attach the accordion folded pages to the inside of each book board piece (front and back covers). The pages can then be decorated as desired. See page 40 for decorating ideas.

I have decorated the pages of my journal as shown below using the following items and techniques. I hope that these ideas will inspire you when making your own memory book.

These are some the techniques I used:

Direct to paper method: I used this technique to age the pages. Use the small ink pads (usually oval in shape) and rub the color directly on the page. In this project, I used four different colors and overlapped them. Experiment with this technique on a separate piece of paper to achieve just the look you're after.

Embossing: This is a process to give stamped images a little dimension and, in some cases, color (see page 3 for instructions on how to emboss). Embossing can also give a metallized or metallic look.

Gel pens: When working on dark paper such as black, I write with gel pens, which are available in a myriad of colors.

Glitter glue: This comes in a pen-like device and is used to highlight an area with glitter. It's less messy than working with loose glitter and glue.

Doors and windows can make your journal really exciting and creative. Note below the gold embossed doors on the third page that open up to display a stamped image of an Egyptian queen. This is simply created using two cut-out pieces of paper glued onto the page. I stamped the doors with an attractive architectural stamp that was then highlighted with gold embossing powder.

Plastic modeling material: I used reptile patterned and gold Friendly Plastic modeling material for this project. I melted them together for the image on the fourth page.

Using found objects: This is the fun part of designing your journal. I used the end piece of a chopstick and a hardware store washer painted gold as the door opener for this journal. Save scraps and bits of paper, fabric, ribbon, and punch-outs from previous projects. Don't throw anything away! I save all of these scraps in zippered plastic bags, some of them filed by color. When I'm designing a new project, I get these bits out and sort through them and see if they'll fit on my current project.

Other embellishments used in this project:

travel related stamps
scrap pieces of paper
charms
sequins
jewels
metallic paints
beads
magazine pictures
color copies (the passport)

CIGAR BOX CHIC

Small purses made out of wooden cigar boxes have become quite popular, selling for over $100 in some specialty stores. It's fun (and much less expensive) to decorate your own cigar box, and create a stylish evening bag for yourself or a friend.

Two pieces of stamped sea glass form the centerpiece of this elegant purse. One displays golden script lettering, while the second

features a glamorous face. Pearlized paper, black velvet, elegant cording and tassels add to a look of utter luxury.

You can improvise your own unique touches and create a purse that's absolutely one-of-a-kind. This project is really special— there's nothing like feeling chic and fashionable wearing your own work of art!

CIGAR BOX CHIC

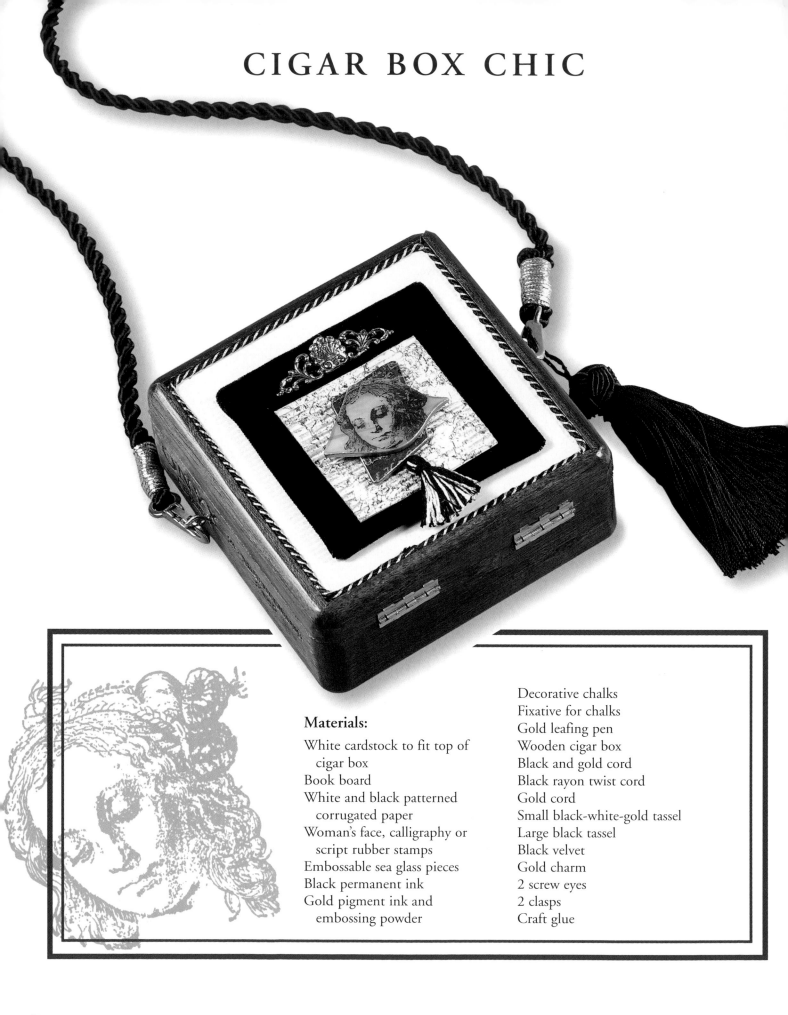

Materials:

White cardstock to fit top of
  cigar box
Book board
White and black patterned
  corrugated paper
Woman's face, calligraphy or
  script rubber stamps
Embossable sea glass pieces
Black permanent ink
Gold pigment ink and
  embossing powder
Decorative chalks
Fixative for chalks
Gold leafing pen
Wooden cigar box
Black and gold cord
Black rayon twist cord
Gold cord
Small black-white-gold tassel
Large black tassel
Black velvet
Gold charm
2 screw eyes
2 clasps
Craft glue

1. Stamp the image of a woman's face on one piece of sea glass using permanent ink. Heat set with a heat gun.

2. Color the face using the chalks. Spray on fixative.

3. Stamp the script image to the other piece of seaglass and emboss with gold. Edge both pieces with the gold leafing pen.

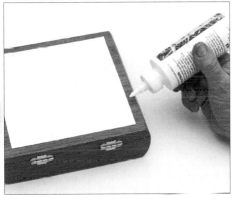

4. Cut the piece of white cardstock to fit the cigar box and glue in place using craft glue.

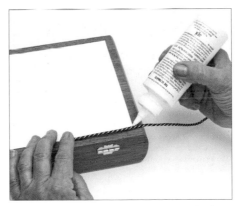

5. Edge the cardstock with the black and gold cord using craft glue.

6. Cover the piece of bookboard with the black velvet and craft glue.

7. Glue a gold charm to the upper part of the black velvet piece. Layer the pieces including the small tassel and the corrugated piece on the cigar box, centering them on the white cardstock (refer to photo). Glue in position.

8. Measure down from the top of the box on each side to position screw eyes. Mark. Twist to screw them into the box.

9. Cut the black cord to desired length, approximately 58" (147cm), for the purse handle. Thread the end of the black cord through the end of the clasp and fold over the cord making a loop. Wrap with gold cord, tie and knot. Glue to secure. Repeat with the other end of the cord. Tie a large tassel to one end of the cord. Attach hooks to the screw eyes.

Pattern for Pocketful of Memories
Page 17

Rubber Stamp Sources

Page 9

Stamps from
Nature Prints
Fred Mullett

Page 12

Stampers Anonymous

Page 14

A Stamp in the Hand

Stampington   Acey Deucy

Rubber Stamp Sources

Page 21

Non Sequiter

Stamp Out Cute

Acey Deucy

Acey Deucy

A Lost Art
not available

Page 23 and 24

Acey Deucy

Acey Deucy

Acey Deucy

Love To Stamp

Acey Deucy

Embossing Arts

Acey Deucy

Post Modern Design

PSX

Page 19 and 20

L'ARTISTE
Tin Can Mail
not available

Stampers Anonymous

Acey Deucy

Stampers Anonymous

Tin Can Mail
not available

Stampers Anonymous

Rubber Poet

Acey Deucy

Stamp Out Cute

Page 28

Love is patient, love is kind. It does not envy, it does not boast, it is not proud. It is not rude, it is not self seeking, it is not easily angered. It does not delight in evil but rejoices in the truth. It always protects, always trusts, always hopes, always perseveres. Love never fails.

Paper Inspirations
1 Cor. 13

Page 32

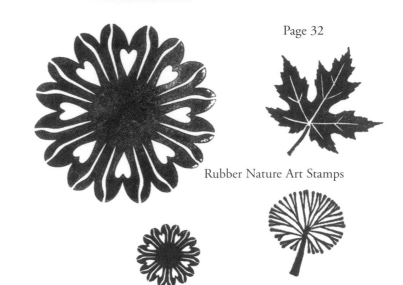

Rubber Nature Art Stamps

Page 34

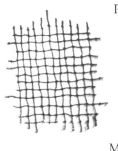

Magenta

Page 37

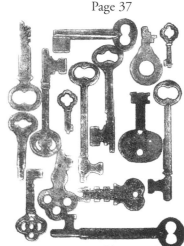

Rubber Monger

River City Rubber Works

Page 40

JudiKins

Peddler's Pack

Just for Fun

Acey Deucy

Stampers Anonymous

Stampers Anonymous

JudiKins

Stampers Anonymous

Page 43

Just for Fun

Acey Deucy

SOURCES

Ink Pads
Clearsnap Inc.
www.clearsnap.com
Cat's Eye, Colorbox, MetaleXtra

Tsukineko Inc.
www.tsukineko.com
Encore metallic ink stamp pads

Markers and Pens
Sakura of America
www.gellyroll.com

Tsukineko Inc.
www.tsukineko.com

Uchida of America
www.uchida.com

Yasutomo
www.yasutomo.com

Embossing Supplies
JudiKins
www.judikins.com
Diamond Glaze
Amazing Glaze
Psycedelic Embossing Powders
Clear embossing ink

Suze Weinberg Design Studio
www.schmoozewithsuze.com
Ultra Thick Embossing Enamel

Clay
American Art Clay
www.amaco.com
Fimo Clay, Friendly Plastics,
other clay supplies

Creative Paperclay
www.paperclay.com
Paper Clay

Sculpey
www.sculpey.com
Polymer Clay

Paints and Stains
Jacquard Products
www.jacquardproducts.com
Lumiere metallic acrylics

Postmodern Designs
405 321-3176
Walnut Ink Crystals

Miscellaneous
Craf-T Products Inc.
www.craftproducts.com
Decorative chalks
Mini Metallic Rub-ons

Gail's Glass
562 425-4679
Embossable sea glass

Magenta
www.magentastyle.com
Framable Art Kits

Glues and Adhesives
Crafter's Pick
520 Cleveland Ave.
Albany, CA 94710
The Ultimate Glue

Gane Bros. & Lane Inc.
Yes Glue
www.ganebrothers.com

Rubber Stamps
Acey Deucy
www.LKPerrella.com

ArtWalk/Rubber Nature ArtStamps
www.rubbernature.com
www.obertinsartwalk.com

Embossing Arts
www.embossingarts.com

JudiKins, Inc.
www.judikins.com

Just For Fun
www.jffstamps.com

Love To Stamp
360 736-9535

Magenta
www.magentastyle.com

Non Sequitur
www.nonsequiturstamps.com

Paper Inspirations
www.paperinspirations.com

The Peddler's Pack
Stampworks
www.pcddlerspack.com
Postmodern Designs
postmoderndesign@aol.com

PSX
www.psxdesign.com

River City Rubber Works
www.rivercityrubberworks.com

Rubber Monger
www.rubbermonger.com

Rubber Poet
www.rubberpoet.com

Stampers Anonymous
The Creative Block
fwww.stampersanonymous.com

Stampington & Co.
www.stampington.com

A Stamp in the Hand
www.astampinthehand.com

Stamp Out Cute
phone/fax 559 323-7174

Stamps from Nature Prints
www.fredmullett.com

Judy's favorite retail stamp store:
A Little Bizaar
31768 Casino Dr. #107B
Lake Elsinore, CA
(909) 471-0882

CREDITS
Produced by
Banar Designs, Inc. / P.O. Box 483 /
Fallbrook, CA 92088
email: banar@earthlink.net
www.banardesigns.com

Art Direction: Barbara Finwall
Editorial Direction: Nancy Javier
Photography: Stephen Whalen
Computer Graphics: Wade Rollins
and Chris Nelsen
Project Direction: Jerilyn Clements
Writing: Susan Borsch
Illustrations: Victoria Dye

Explore the Exciting World of Rubber Stamps with North Light Books!

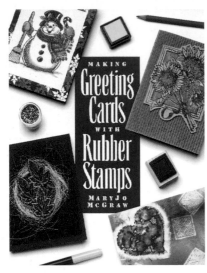

Here are hundreds of colorful ideas and techniques for creating one-of-a-kind greetings—from the elegant to the festive to the downright goofy—all in a matter of minutes! Try your hand at any of the 30 step-by-step projects inside or take off in your own original direction.
ISBN 0-89134-713-5, paperback, 128 pages, #30821-K

Use rubber stamps to decorate candles, jewelry, purses, book covers, wall hangings and more. 16 step-by-step projects show you how by using creative techniques, surfaces and embellishments, including metal, beads, embossing powder and clay—even shrink plastic!
ISBN 1-58180-128-9, paperback, 128 pages, #31829-K

Filled with fresh designs, simple techniques and gorgeous colors, this exciting book combines two fun, easy-to-master crafts in one. You'll find guidelines for stamping images on all your clay creations, including jewelry, home décor and more, along with advice for experimenting with color and finish. The wide variety of projects guarantees spontaneous, delightful results.
ISBN 1-58180-155-6, paperback, 128 pages, #31904-K

Let Sandra McCall show you how to make gorgeous rubber stamp treasures in 30 minutes or less. From home décor and party favors to desk accessories and wearable gifts, you'll find 27 exciting projects inside. Each one is easy to do and inexpensive to make—perfect for those days when you want to create something quick!
ISBN 1-58180-271-4, paperback, 128 pages, #32142-K

These books and other fine North Light titles are available from your local art & craft retailer, bookstore, online supplier or by calling 1-800-448-0915.